PARANORMAL
INVESTIGATIONS

Aliens, UFOs,
and Unexplained Encounters

Andrew Coddington

New York

Library of Congress Cataloging-in-Publication Data

Names: Coddington, Andrew, author.
Title: Aliens, UFOs, and unexplained encounters / Andrew Coddington.
Description: New York : Cavendish Square Publishing, 2018. |
Series: Paranormal investigations | Includes bibliographical references and index.
Identifiers: LCCN 2016048567 (print) | LCCN 2016050263 (ebook) |
ISBN 9781502628459 (library bound) | ISBN 9781502628466 (E-book)
Subjects: LCSH: Unidentified flying objects--Juvenile literature. |
Life on other planets--Juvenile literature. | Extraterrestrial beings--Juvenile literature.
Classification: LCC TL789.2 .C634 2017 (print) | LCC TL789.2 (ebook) |
DDC 001.942--dc23
LC record available at HYPERLINK "https://lccn.loc.gov/2016048567" https://lccn.loc.gov/2016048567

Editorial Director: David McNamara
Editor: Kristen Susienka
Copy Editor: Rebecca Rohan
Associate Art Director: Amy Greenan
Designer: Joseph Macri
Production Coordinator: Karol Szymczuk
Photo Research: J8 Media

The photographs in this book are used by permission and through the courtesy of: Cover ThePalmer/E+/Getty Images; p. 4 Look and Learn/Bridgeman Images; p. 7 Stefano Bianchetti/Corbis/Getty Images; p. 8 Bananaboy/Shutterstock.com; p. 10 Seo75/Wikimedia Commons/File:Yowie-statue-Kilcoy-Queensland.JPG/CC BY SA 2.1; p. 13 George Rinhart/Corbis/Getty Images; p. 16 Gudkov Andrey/Shutterstock.com; p. 18 Bettmann/Corbis/Getty Images; p. 21 Micael Carlsson/Moment/Getty Images; p. 22 AP Images; p. 25 Dale O'Dell/Alamy Stock Photo; p. 28 MichaelTaylor3d/Shutterstock.com; p. 30 Photo Researchers/Alamy Stock Photo; p. 33 Keystone-France/Gamma-Rapho via Getty Images; p. 35 Mary Evans Picture Library/Alamy Stock Photo; p. 38 Fortean/TopFoto/The Image Works; p. 41 Rolls Press/Popperfoto/Getty Images; p. 42 Fortean/Topham/The Image Works; p. 43 Designua/Shutterstock.com; p. 46 Lightpoet/Shutterstock.com; pp. 48-49 AF Archive/Alamy Stock Photo; p. 51 Lian Deng/Shutterstock.com; p. 55 Teri Virbickis/Shutterstock.com.

Printed in the United States of America

Contents

UFOs, or "unidentified flying objects," have been spotted in the skies practically since the beginning of history, leaving many people to wonder what they are.

Space: The Final Frontier

The universe is an enormous place. Earth is just one of several planets orbiting around our sun, which, despite being 875,000 miles (1.4 million kilometers) across and large enough to hold well over a million Earths, is still just an average-sized star. It is one of many such stars in our **galaxy**, the Milky Way. In fact, there are approximately one hundred billion such stars in the Milky Way alone, and about as many other galaxies with about as many stars in the entire universe—that is, in the parts that we have observed.

The Universe and Others Out There

Scientists estimate the universe to be fourteen billion years old. Many believe that the universe was created by the big bang, a theoretical event during which all the matter in the universe, compressed into a unimaginably dense, unimaginably hot ball of mass, suddenly exploded. It formed all of the interstellar clouds of gas—stars and nebulas—and hulks of rock—planets—now in the universe in the process. Residual energy from this explosion continues to radiate today, which means our universe is always expanding and, theoretically, forming new galaxies, stars, and planets along the way.

There is a practically infinite number of stars in the universe, and each undiscovered system could bear the possibility of alien life.

As if the universe were not already big enough, however, many scientists hypothesize that our universe may not even be the only one. In fact, there may be dozens, hundreds, thousands, or even millions or more **multiverses** existing alongside one another, each perhaps equally as large as or larger than our own.

Given all this *space*, many people, including some of the world's most famous scientists, believe it is not only possible but likely for life to exist somewhere else in the universe besides Earth. Life as we know it on Earth requires certain "building blocks" called elements, such as carbon, hydrogen, oxygen, nitrogen, and others, as well as certain circumstances—a hospitable environment, for example—in order to survive and thrive. Recently, scientists operating remote-controlled space explorers have discovered that the landscapes of certain bodies within our own solar system, such as Mars and the moon Enceladus, which orbits Saturn, feature flowing water, which is widely thought to support life. In the case of Mars, it seems likely that the Red Planet may once have supported basic organisms such as bacteria. Outside our solar system, there may be many more places that support basic life, as well as "Goldilocks" planets where the circumstances are just right to support more advanced organisms and maybe even civilizations.

Extraterrestrial Life

The expansiveness of the universe has served as a sandbox for the human imagination practically since man first looked up at the night sky and wondered what was behind the scattered pinpricks of light. The way in which the universe warps our sense of distance and time sparked one of the most famous lines in modern culture: "A long time ago in a

Aliens such as these from George Lucas's Star Wars series have captured Earthlings' imaginations for centuries.

galaxy far, far away." In *Star Wars*, George Lucas conceived of a system of planets and stars where advanced creatures of all shapes and sizes routinely travel vast distances with ease. Although science has yet to validate the existence of advanced **extraterrestrial** civilizations outside our solar system, there is no doubt in the minds of many that they exist, that they have the technology to explore the deepest corners of the universe, and that they are here, now, closely studying the movements of humanity.

HOW PROBABLE IS ALIEN LIFE?

Scientists have struggled to find a way to measure the likelihood of alien life in the universe. Many, including some of the world's most prominent scientists, believe that since the universe is practically infinite, alien life is not just possible but likely. However, the scale of the universe also poses a scientific conundrum, because there is so much about it that we don't understand. These two approaches lead many scientists to believe that anything must be possible, but also cause many others to argue that we just can't know for sure.

In order to help address this problem, Dr. Frank Drake, an astronomer at the University of California at Santa Cruz, came up with an equation in 1961 to calculate the possibility of making contact with an intelligent alien life force in our own galaxy. Drake's equation, as it became known, defined what sorts of variables must be in play in order for a system to support life. Among these are the number of stars that are neither too hot nor too cool—"Goldilocks stars"—and might thereby support life, the number of stars that host orbiting planets like our own system, the number of planets in that system that can sustain life, and so on. Although Drake's equation does not state whether life outside Earth exists, it is meant to be a framework for thinking about the possibility of alien life scientifically.

Many UFOs are described as silvery discs capable of flying at high speeds.

CHAPTER ONE

UFOs in History

Sightings of unidentified flying objects, also known as **UFOs**, are commonplace, in part because the term "UFO" does not necessarily indicate an airborne object of extraterrestrial origin commanded by little green men. Anything traveling in the sky that is not immediately identifiable qualifies as a UFO. This might include rare but natural atmospheric events, such as the phenomenon known as ball lightning or swamp gas, or ordinary man-made objects, such as weather balloons and experimental aircraft.

During the Cold War, for example, many **alleged** sightings of UFOs happened near United States airbases where aircraft were being tested. Among these was the U-2, a jet-propelled plane designed to travel at extremely high altitudes in order to run reconnaissance missions in the air above enemy bases and missile installations. The U-2 is capable of traveling at up to 70,000 feet (21,336 meters), or just on the edge of the atmosphere. (By comparison, most commercial airplanes only travel between 40,000 and 45,000 feet (12,192–13,716 m).) To ordinary civilians at the time, witnessing a plane flying at that altitude was considered impossible, which led many to question whether or not it was man-made. Because the aircraft's design and purpose were top secret, the United States government remained silent about the true identity of the U-2 for many years in order to protect the integrity of its mission.

Ball lightning is a rare but natural phenomenon that may explain many cases of UFO sightings.

The majority of UFOs have mundane explanations, but there remain a large number of UFO sightings not so easily accounted for. These have come from a variety of sources ranging in credibility, from common civilians to pilots who witness unusual lights or even aircraft during their flights, to high-ranking military officials expressing concern over airborne vehicles that do not seem to have any reasonable human explanation.

Ancient Aliens

Ancient literature is full of chapters that prove intriguing for students of UFO history. This seems to suggest that the presence of unidentified aircraft is as old as history itself. One such instance comes from the Greek biographer Plutarch,

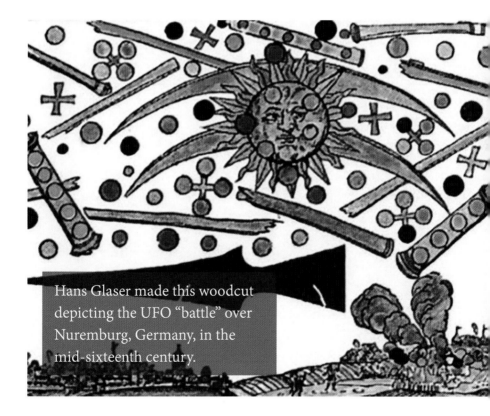

Hans Glaser made this woodcut depicting the UFO "battle" over Nuremburg, Germany, in the mid-sixteenth century.

who, despite saying he was not a strict historian, is widely considered one of the best sources for the history of ancient Greece and Rome. In his book *Lucullus*, Plutarch writes of a bizarre episode that took place before a battle in 74 BCE. According to Plutarch, moments before the two armies were about to engage, "the sky burst asunder, and a huge, flame-like body was seen to fall between the two armies. In shape, it was most like a wine-jar, and in color, like molten silver. Both sides were astonished at the sight," Plutarch notes, "and separated."

While the UFO in Plutarch's book may have inspired peace to the humans who witnessed it, a later historical instance of a UFO encounter seems to have been of a far more violent nature. On April 14, 1561, the sky above Nuremberg, Germany, was the site of what many witnesses considered to be a battle between strange aircraft. The event was documented by Hans Glaser, an artist living in Nuremberg, who supposedly witnessed the event. This inspired him to publish a report and a woodcut of the battle in a broadsheet, which is what we might consider a tabloid today. This ancient "artist's rendering" shows dozens of crosses, discs, cylinders, and spikes charging at one another before the morning sun. The "dreadful apparition" disturbed the whole town. Citizens took the event to be a warning from God.

Modern Sightings

The number of sightings of UFOs increased in the twentieth century. This is in part because that century witnessed the invention of the airplane. Aviation technology improved at an exponential rate in the twentieth century, seeing the development of military and commercial aircraft, as well as

The desolate Nevada State Route 375 has been the site of numerous UFO sightings, leading to the nickname the "Extraterrestrial Highway."

spacecraft like satellites and the International Space Station. All this time in the air meant that humans were closer to and more exposed to aerial phenomena. Today, sightings continue. Camera technology has improved greatly, so if a person witnesses a UFO, they likely have immediate access to technology capable of capturing high-quality images. That's a far cry from Glaser's fanciful woodcut of the "UFO battle" over Nuremberg.

The importance of airplanes and portable camera technology in the study of UFOs was proven as early as the mid-twentieth century, when pilots fighting during World War II witnessed unexplained aerial phenomena during operations over both the European and Pacific battlefields. Nicknamed "foo fighters," these aircraft were reported by pilots to be bright, silvery objects without wings or tails. These aircraft were capable of reaching high speeds as well as conducting seemingly impossible maneuvers. In one case, a Royal Air Force fighter pilot patrolling over France was chased by two bright lights that followed his every move while maintaining a precise distance from one another. Whether these UFOs were experimental aircraft, a natural phenomenon known as ball lightning, or something else entirely, has never been proven.

The foo fighters of World War II closely resemble the typical "flying saucer," but recent sightings of UFOs are not limited to disc-shaped objects. Contemporary UFOs take a variety of shapes, especially cylinders and triangles with lights at each corner.

Experimental aircraft, such as this German V-2 rocket from World War II, are often subjects of UFO sightings.

Few UFO sightings have ever reached the notoriety as the one that occurred at Roswell, New Mexico, in July 1947. On Independence Day, several Roswell residents reported seeing a bright, disc-shaped object flying quickly through the sky. In fact, the military had also been observing an unidentified flying object for days. On the morning of July 5, two locals named William Brazel and Timothy Proctor

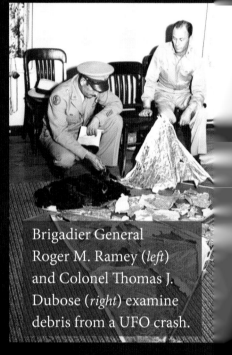

Brigadier General Roger M. Ramey (*left*) and Colonel Thomas J. Dubose (*right*) examine debris from a UFO crash.

came across a pile of debris, including rubber, splintered wood, and unusually lightweight but flexible metal foil, in a grazing field. The discovery was reported to the sheriff, who in turn involved the military stationed at the Roswell Army Air Force Base. Those who initially investigated the discovery were baffled, which led the press to issue a statement claiming that a flying disc had crash-landed at Roswell. Eventually, a mysterious unidentified government agency commanded the press to stop circulating the story. Later, the military released a statement claiming a downed weather balloon had been recovered.

The mysterious cover-up at Roswell has sparked UFO speculation ever since, with many **conspiracy theorists** arguing that the debris came not from a weather balloon but from an extraterrestrial spacecraft. They're right—at least in part. Although the events at Roswell indicate the existence of an official government cover-up, the debris did not come from an alien spaceship any more than it did a weather balloon. The government later revealed the details of a covert operation called Project Mogul, which employed reconnaissance balloons very similar in appearance to weather balloons in order to gather atmospheric data on Soviet missile tests. The debris found at Roswell belonged to one of these balloons, which had unexpectedly crash-landed and whose discovery was suppressed in order to protect Project Mogul. Nevertheless, the official explanation has not satisfied some people, who believe that Roswell was the subject of a conspiracy and that the government will not reveal its knowledge of alien life.

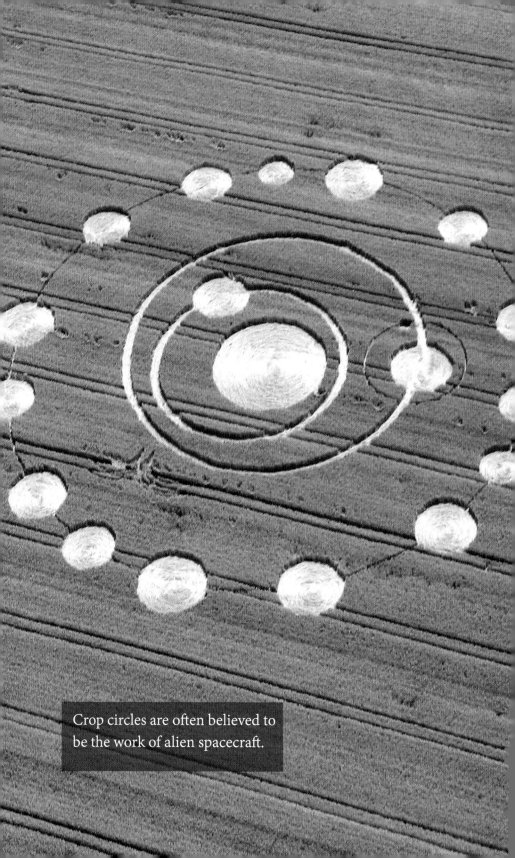

Crop circles are often believed to
be the work of alien spacecraft.

CHAPTER TWO

Investigating UFOs

In the late 1960s, members of the American Institute of Aeronautics and Astronautics suggested the formation of a scientific body to review UFO reports. As a result, the Technical Committee on Atmospheric Environment and the Technical Committee on Space and Atmospheric Physics joined forces in 1967, forming a UFO subcommittee. From the beginning, the UFO subcommittee encountered a number of issues and described "a maze of preconceptions, emotions, bias, hasty conclusions, and excessive and misleading publicity." In its report published in November 1970, the subcommittee realized that it would never be able to offer a satisfactory and conclusive answer to the question of UFOs and extraterrestrial life. Instead, the subcommittee said, they undertook the task of determining whether or not there was any scientifically significant problem and to advise scientists and the government of their conclusion.

The subcommittee found that there were, at the time, approximately twenty thousand documented cases of UFO sightings, but that those accounted for only 5 to 15 percent of total cases, with the vast majority going unreported. Despite the limited availability of cases, however, the subcommittee argued that the number was large enough to be significant.

Reports of a crashed "flying saucer" in Roswell, New Mexico, sparked a media firestorm.

Of these cases, the subcommittee found that less than 5 percent qualified as **hoaxes**, 75 percent could be reasonably explained, and between 15 and 20 percent were insufficiently documented. "In other words," the subcommittee wrote, "what may appear to the untrained observer as strange and unexplainable is in most cases known and explainable."

Despite this, the subcommittee found a "small residue of well-documented but unexplainable cases … characterized by both a high degree of credibility and a high abnormality." This poses a problem: should we assume that these few cases have natural causes because the majority of UFO cases do, or are these cases unexplained because they were caused by something we do not understand?

At the end of the report, the subcommittee recommended that the scientific organizations, the government, and the public take a "wait-and-see" approach as more data is collected. However, the subcommittee stressed the need for scientists and government officials to rationally consider proposals on the topic without bias, saying that this recommendation constitutes "perhaps our most important conclusion."

The reality behind UFOs has a lot to do with the trustworthiness of the source reporting the event. History has shown that many alleged sightings were simply hoaxes, or fakes, made by people hoping to gain fame. That's why evaluating a sighting often begins with a look at the person reporting it, since their motives often influence how the story is received. However, many people who believe in the existence of flying objects of extraterrestrial origin make the argument that the possibility of bias does not necessarily preclude the truthfulness of a witness.

UFOlogy

The study of UFOs is commonly called **UFOlogy**, the first recorded use of which occurred in the *Times Literary Supplement* in 1959. Unlike biology, chemistry, physics, psychology, or any other scientific fields, one would be hard pressed to find a Department of UFOlogy at a university or a peer-reviewed article in a scientific research magazine. This is because conventional science tends to view UFOlogy as a **pseudoscience**, or false science, in large part because many UFOlogists do not rely on the scientific method, the tried and tested procedure that humans have used to study and understand the world around us. The scientific method begins with a hypothesis. It is then tested through carefully controlled experiments, the results of which are observed and recorded, leading to either the confirmation or the modification of the original hypothesis. Many opponents of UFOlogy argue that it does not qualify as a true science because its researchers typically begin with the conclusion and seek to explain its results retroactively. This might lead UFOlogists to ignore certain variables or put too much faith in far-flung explanations. For this reason, UFOlogists are often stigmatized by the scientific community.

UFOlogists, for their part, reject this stigma. They believe their field of study to be a rigorous and academic pursuit on par with any other science. A UFOlogist might argue that the reliance on conclusions as the starting point for their inquiries is a limitation of their objects of study. UFOs often appear at inconvenient times and without warning, and their appearance cannot be replicated. Because of the very nature of UFOs, it is impossible to design the type of controlled experiments that are able to be repeated. However, many of the problems associated with studying UFOs are also shared by the field of meteorology. Like UFOs, meteorological events are often unexpected and are impossible to recreate in controlled lab environments, yet meteorology is a respected scientific field. No one denies the existence of tornadoes, even those who have never seen one in person, a UFOlogist might say. So, why not UFOs?

Types of Evidence

Alleged UFOs have been seen since the beginning of history—and may even predate recorded human history by some time. However, because of the longstanding stigma attached to the study of UFOs and aliens by the more conventional sciences, UFOlogy has struggled to gather the kind of talented and analytical minds needed to sort fact from fiction.

There are a variety of types of evidence of UFOs that help to categorize sightings and rank them in order of believability. The first type of evidence is the most common and also the least trustworthy: eyewitness reports. There have been countless purported sightings of UFOs by individuals, but these are generally considered unreliable because of the limitations of the human body or the possibility that a person's state of mind might be negatively affected by things such as alcohol and drugs, fear, mental illness, or even just lack of knowledge.

To explore the limits of eyewitness accounts, let's explore this common UFO sighting scenario as an example: While out one night, a person spots a very bright light traveling quickly in one direction before suddenly changing direction. Before they can take a picture of the light with the camera that they're carrying, the object vanishes.

On its face, this report may seem compelling. However, because this comes from an eyewitness with no additional evidence, it's important to look at their story more closely to be sure there isn't a rational explanation. This story is immediately questionable because it takes place at night. Humans' eyesight has not evolved to see clearly in the dark, which means that our eyes struggle to make out fine detail or accurately judge size or distance at night. Additionally, there is the question of whether or not the person was under the influence of drugs or alcohol at the time or if they suffer from a mental illness. Even if we can answer those questions, there is the possibility that their mind might have played a trick on them, seeing something that wasn't actually there because it was influenced by a television show, movie, or story about aliens and UFOs. Another important question to ask is whether or not the witness has anything to gain by coming forward. Many alleged UFO sightings later confirmed as hoaxes were thrown into question because the original witness had been proven to be after fame or a monetary reward.

Once those questions have been cleared up, and the investigator is confident the witness was not impaired or

THE DELPHOS RING

One of the most intriguing and well-documented cases of a UFO encounter occurred on November 2, 1971, in the small town of Delphos, Kansas. That evening, sixteen-year-old Ronnie Johnson was working on his family's farm when he noticed a squat, mushroom-shaped object hovering 2 feet (0.6 m) off the ground a short distance from where he was standing. As Ronnie approached it, he noticed that it was making a noise like the rhythmic banging of the drum of an old washing machine, before it took off, briefly blinding him.

When his eyes readjusted, Ronnie ran to the house to tell his parents. They went to the place where Ronnie had seen the object and noticed a faintly glowing ring in the grass beneath where the object had been hovering. They took a Polaroid photo of it, and Ronnie's mother and father both touched the material, which caused their fingers to go numb for a short time.

The next day, a local reporter visited the site and noted that the ring had ceased to glow but that there was now a doughnut-shaped circle of bare earth as well as a fallen tree and some broken limbs nearby.

The Delphos ring incident is one of the most compelling cases of a UFO, primarily because it blends so many examples of evidence, including multiple eyewitness accounts. In addition to the Johnsons, a man in a neighboring town reported seeing a light traveling at approximately the same place and time as the event at the Johnsons' farm. There is also photographic and physical **trace evidence** of the ring.

So, does this case prove the existence of UFOs? Not necessarily. Certain aspects of the case may have natural explanations. The mysterious glowing ring from which the case gets its name was found to have been the location where a chicken feed station had once stood. It is possible that the droppings from those chickens may have altered the chemical composition of the soil around it, leading to an unusual ring where grass did not grow. Further, an analysis of the soil was found to host a certain type of fungus, some species of which grow in circles known as "fairy rings," can have incandescent properties, and can release spores that can affect a person's health. Lastly, there is some question surrounding the Johnsons' motives. At that time, the tabloid the *National Enquirer* had issued a public statement offering a reward to anyone who could present compelling evidence of a UFO. A reporter from that paper had approached the Johnsons and given them $5,000 for their story.

influenced in some way and legitimately did see something, there are still an overwhelming number of rational explanations for the mysterious light that the witness may not have considered. There are countless man-made and natural sources of lights in the sky, from aircraft, satellites, and spacecraft to lightning, candescent atmospheric gases, and even bright celestial bodies such as the moon or Mercury.

But what if the person had managed to take a picture of a UFO before it vanished? Photographs and video recordings are another type of evidence that UFOlogists and **skeptics** often use to prove or disprove the presence of UFOs in our skies. Although it tends to add more credibility to an eyewitness account, photographic evidence is also full of problems for UFO researchers. There is no shortage of photos and videos taken of alleged extraterrestrial spacecraft, with some dating as far back as the invention of the camera. Although it may seem that this abundance of photographic evidence must surely point to the

It is not always easy to tell whether a UFO photo is real.

existence of UFOs, the overwhelming majority of these are not reliable. For one thing, camera technology, like the human senses of observation, is limited. In order to produce a clear, detailed picture at a distance, a photographer hoping to capture a UFO must have a sophisticated, expensive, and bulky zoom lens. The lens must be carefully focused in order to produce a clear picture, which isn't always a possibility when an unexpected flying object cruises into view without warning. On top of this, a picture—be it film or a digital file—can be corrupted, producing shapes and images that weren't there when the photo was originally taken. Furthermore, as with eyewitness reports, there is always the possibility that an image has been deliberately faked in order to stir up a hoax. This has only become easier with the growth of digital cameras and photo editing software such as Photoshop.

More convincing proof than eyewitness accounts and photographs belong to a category that might be called physical trace evidence. Trace evidence tends to be more convincing than either eyewitness testimony or photographic evidence because it is physical, which means that it can be handled and examined by investigators well after an alleged UFO encounter. Leftover evidence also means that it is generally more difficult for would-be hoaxers to assemble and stage, requiring a greater investment in time and resources. One of the most common categories of trace evidence includes changes in the environment. Environmental evidence might consist of marks or burns in the ground left by, say, the landing gear or exhaust of an extraterrestrial craft, or branches or trees that have been broken or knocked over by a spaceship.

A more rare and puzzling example of physical proof includes evidence left on the bodies of alleged witnesses. Doctors or nurses cannot explain the cause of some of these marks.

CROP CIRCLES: FACT OR FICTION?

Probably the most famous (or infamous) example of physical evidence left by UFOs are crop circles. As their name suggests, crop circles appear in fields where sections have been flattened to form a particular design. These tend to follow a circular shape or pattern, but they have also been found to follow complicated mathematical patterns, such as fractals, as well as representations of things found on Earth, especially insects. As perplexing as crop circles may seem, many have been confirmed hoaxes. Working under the cover of darkness, an individual or a team of people can easily create a crop circle by flattening the crop using a board with a rope attached to either end. However, some crop circles remain mysterious, in many cases because investigators examining them have found the stalks chemically altered to form the pattern rather than physically broken as would happen with a human hoaxer.

Close Encounters

In 1972, astronomer and UFOlogist J. Allen Hynek published *The UFO Experience: A Scientific Inquiry*, in which he proposed a scale to rate and classify sightings of UFOs. Hynek's scale is based primarily on the distance between an alleged UFO and a witness, ranking the sightings in order of least to most reliable. The least reliable category of sightings is called distant encounters, or "DE," which take place at a distance greater than 500 feet (152 m). Within this category, the least reliable type of sightings are nocturnal lights (classified DE-I), which are unusual lights spotted in the night sky. These are considered least reliable because the distance of observation coupled with the limited abilities of a human to see clearly at night increases the likelihood that a mundane object or phenomenon might be mistaken for a UFO. After nocturnal lights, there are daytime discs (DE-II), which are UFOs seen in daylight. These are considered to be more reliable than nocturnal lights but are still suspect. The last type of sighting within the distant encounters category is radar-visual sightings (DE-III), in which a visual sighting is further corroborated by an unexpected object registering on radar, which would suggest that the object has physicality and is not just a rare but natural light phenomenon. Radar-visual sightings are relatively rare, as they require a witness as well as a radar array, which few ordinary people have access to.

After distant encounters, there are **close encounters**, or "CE." All close encounters take place within 500 feet (152 m), which lend them an additional credibility due to the short distance at which they are observed. As with distant encounters, close encounters are ranked in order of least to most reliable. Close encounters of the first kind (CE-I) are the most basic and include sightings where one or more witnesses observe a UFO at a close distance, but the UFO does not seem to interact with the environment in any way. Following this first category are close encounters of the second kind (CE-II). Such occurrences include sightings as well as trace evidence, ranging from electronic or mechanical interference with man-made devices (such as a car ignition failing to start or a radio or cell phone experiencing unexplained static) to marks left on the ground (such as burns or indentations) to effects on plants, animals, or humans (such as burns on the skin). The final category is close encounters of the thirdkind (CE-III), which are defined by witnessing an occupant of a UFO—in other words, an alien.

J. ALLEN HYNEK

J. Allen Hynek

The most recognizable name associated with UFO research is J. Allen Hynek. Hynek was born into a family of Czechoslovakian immigrants on May 1, 1910, in Chicago. He studied at the University of Chicago, earning first his bachelor of science degree and then a PhD in 1935. He worked as a physics and astronomy professor and later dean until he became involved with the military at Wright-Patterson Air Force Base in Dayton, Ohio, in 1948. There he consulted on investigations into reports of UFOs. His work eventually contributed to the development of Project Blue Book, a series of classified investigations into UFOs by the Air Force, in 1952.

Throughout the next two decades, Hynek continued to add impressive credentials to his résumé, including helping to establish the worldwide network of tracking stations for the United States's first artificial satellite, developing a telescope that incorporated the new television technology at the time, and accepting a chairmanship at Northwestern University's astronomy department.

After Project Blue Book was closed in 1969, Hynek continued to advocate for the burgeoning field of UFOlogy, becoming its chief proponent. In 1966, he founded the Center for UFO Studies in Evanston, Illinois (later relocated to Chicago), which provided support to law enforcement officers investigating UFOs. In 1972, he published *The UFO Experience*, in which he proposed his scientific scale for categorizing UFO encounters. He died in 1986 of brain cancer.

Many people claim to have not only seen an alien spacecraft but to have been abducted, or taken.

CHAPTER THREE

Close(r) Encounters

hinking back to J. Allen Hynek's original scale of UFO encounters discussed in chapter 2, it ended at Close Encounters of the Third Kind, which includes sightings close enough to recognize a pilot or other passenger of a UFO. Simply observing an alien at a distance qualifies as a CE-III, but accounts of more personal interaction would also qualify as a CE-III according to Hynek's original scale. However, given that claims of Third Kind Encounters have increased both in number and scope of experience, some UFOlogists have suggested expanding Hynek's scale in order to further quantify such experiences. In these UFOlogists' opinion, the scale should include Fourth, Fifth, Sixth, and even Seventh Kind Close Encounters.

Other Encounters

A Fourth Kind Encounter (CE-IV) would include instances where an individual is **abducted** or detained by aliens, in many cases allegedly, to have medical tests performed on them. CE-V would include direct communication between aliens and humans, and CE-VI would include communication or interaction where permanent harm has been done to a human, including death. Lastly, Close Encounters of the Seventh Kind has been proposed to include cases where an extraterrestrial has mated with or otherwise impregnated a human being for the purposes of producing a human-alien hybrid, also called a "star child," which is outlandish, to say the least. The additions of the Close Encounters categories to Hynek's scale strike many people as bizarre impossibilities, and many in the UFOlogy community seem ready to discard them as such. UFOlogists have not widely accepted any of these new categories, as many believe they undermine Hynek's original scale and its efforts to enforce greater academic rigor on the study of UFOs.

Descriptions of Aliens

There are plenty of cases of people witnessing unexplained aerial phenomena. Far more rare are instances where people see, communicate, or are even taken by extraterrestrial beings. However, these cases have been on the rise over the last century, though it is unclear whether or not actual instances have increased in number or if those who see them are more comfortable in talking about them than they once were.

These cases present an interesting depiction of alien life forms. Although fictional depictions of aliens vary widely, with bizarre combinations of body parts of terrestrial animals, alleged firsthand encounters generally feature more or less the same creature.

"Real life" aliens tend to be humanoid in shape, with two arms and two legs attached to a torso and a head. Their faces tend to be humanoid as well, with eyes, noses, and mouths in a regular arrangement. However, these beings differ from humans in some significant ways. First, they tend to be smaller in stature than an average human, usually 3 feet

THE AURORA ALIEN

The American West in the nineteenth century was a wild place, full of panhandlers, bootleggers, gunslingers—and aliens ... at least according to the *Dallas Morning News*. In a newspaper article from April 19, 1897, an "airship" traveling above the town of Aurora, Texas, crashed into a windmill owned by the local judge. The collision sparked a massive fireball, "scattering debris over several acres of ground, wrecking the windmill and water tank and destroying the judge's flower garden."

The pilot of the craft was later discovered among the wreckage, and although the body was badly mangled, the *Morning News* wrote that he "was not an inhabitant of this world." The body was later buried in the Aurora cemetery, its location noted by an anonymous grave marker. Modern researchers have petitioned the town to allow them to exhume the body to no avail. A team from the show *UFO Hunters* did manage to scan the site with ground-penetrating radar and discovered the presence of a body, though it was too deteriorated to allow any further conclusion of whether or not it was human.

(0.9 m) in height, although some witnesses have reported much taller aliens, including some that are well above the average height of a human. They are also described as rather thin, with long, spindly arms, legs, and fingers, and short torsos. Their skin tends to be gray, though some have also been reported as appearing green, hence the nickname "little green men." Lastly, their facial features tend to differ from regular humans. Most descriptions of extraterrestrials include large almond-shaped eyes that lack irises and are jet black. Their mouths and nostrils are often described as slits in the face, which has no lips or nose. Their heads are also often described as disproportionately large.

Abductions

A few people claim to have even more personal encounters than simply witnessing an alien being from afar. Some say they have been forcibly taken and examined by such creatures. These events, known as abductions, are among the rarest reports of UFO encounters. Although many have been proven to be fanciful delusions of individuals suffering mental illnesses, as with UFO sightings, many cases of alleged alien abductions defy explanation.

One of the first instances of an alien abduction to garner widespread attention was the case of Barney and Betty Hill. In September 1961, the Hills were traveling to their home in New Hampshire after a vacation in Canada. At some point during the night, the Hills noticed an unusually bright object shining in the sky, which they initially thought was a star. They pulled off to the side of the road to get a better look. Mr. Hill saw through a pair of binoculars that the object seemed to be shaped like an oval, with multiple rows of different-colored lights and windows. The Hills were startled by the aircraft, so they got in their car and sped away. A little while later, they arrived home, but something didn't feel right to them. They checked the time and discovered it was two hours later than they thought.

Later that week, the Hills started to have nightmares about being kidnapped and operated on. Disturbed by the recurring dreams, they sought psychiatric help. Under the direction of their doctor, the Hills participated in

DISSECTING A HOAX

Despite being one of the most infamous cases of a UFO encounter, evidence from the Roswell Incident of 1947 did little to confirm the existence of alien life. But then, in 1995, a black-and-white film seeming to depict the autopsy of the body of an extraterrestrial recovered from the Roswell crash surfaced. The video shows the body of a small, humanoid-shaped creature with gouges and burn marks, apparently suffered from the impact of the crash, which is carefully dissected by an anonymous doctor wearing a full-bodied chemical protection suit.

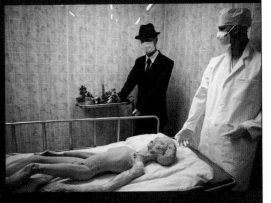

As compelling as the video may be, not everything is as it would seem. Many skeptics and UFOlogists immediately called the video a hoax. The military-style ID number shown at the beginning, allegedly to catalog the video, was proven to be nonsense; the injuries on the alien were inconsistent with a crash landing; and the doctor was shown to have used the dissection tools in a decidedly nonmedical way. Later, a special effects creator named John Humphreys came forward to admit that he had faked the video, saying that he had molded the body out of latex and performed the role of the masked surgeon himself.

hypnosis. While under the effects of their treatment, the Hills described how the object they had seen in the sky landed. Odd-looking men came out of it and dragged them, kicking and screaming, back into the craft. Then, they said, the creatures began to perform medical tests on them separately, before returning them to their car and sending them back on their way.

For the time being, the Hills had only shared their story with their family, close friends, and doctor. However, it was leaked to the *Boston Traveler* four years later, setting off a media firestorm. The account of the Hills' abduction quickly reached every corner of the United States. Even serious UFOlogists commented on the disturbing nature of the Hills' description of their encounter.

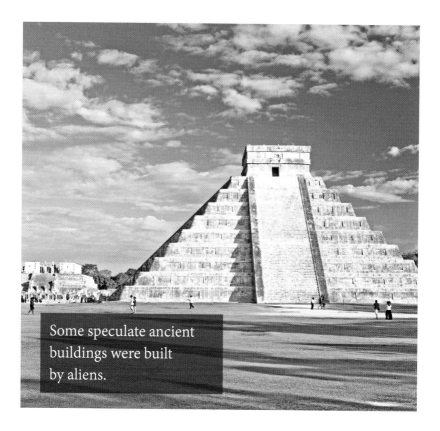

Some speculate ancient buildings were built by aliens.

ANCIENT ALIEN ARCHITECTS?

There is a theory among certain UFOlogists, including Erich von Decker, author of *Chariots of the Gods*, that some of the greatest architectural wonders of the ancient world, such as the Egyptian and Mayan pyramids or the megalithic arrangement at Stonehenge, could not possibly have been built by those civilizations. The Egyptians and Celts, for example, lacked the technology of wheels, which would have made carting stones weighing upwards of 2.5 tons (2.3 metric tons) a monumental if not impossible task. Instead, these UFOlogists argue, extraterrestrial beings must have given ancient peoples the engineering knowledge and tools necessary to craft these structures. This theory has appeared on such popular TV shows as the History Channel's *Ancient Aliens*.

This theory is widely considered laughable by most archaeologists, engineers, and other scientists. The ancient astronaut theory, as it is called, fails to take into account the resourcefulness, intelligence, and inventiveness of ancient cultures. Evidence has shown that ancient cultures possessed both a sophisticated knowledge of mathematics and engineering as well the mechanical know-how and manpower required to build these wonders. In the case of the Egyptian pyramids, for instance, Dutch archaeologists have discovered that the Egyptians used sleds pulled by teams of slaves, which were helped along by other slaves applying a constant slurry of wet sand that significantly reduced the amount of force needed to transport and place the stone blocks.

The possibility of crossing the expanse of the universe is still only theoretical for humans.

CHAPTER FOUR

Exploring the Physics of Extraterrestrial Life

Extraterrestrial life forms are every bit a mystery. For one thing, we are not even sure they exist. On top of that, proposing to study UFOs and aliens is fraught with methodological issues—not to mention professional liabilities, as many would-be UFOlogists are discouraged from the field because it is considered by most scientists to be too far "out there." Nevertheless, the fact remains that there are a number of well-documented encounters that defy normal explanations. What are we to make of those cases? Are these instances of alien involvement here on Earth? To many, the answer would be yes. In the words of Sherlock Holmes, "when you have eliminated the impossible, whatever remains, however improbable, must be the truth." However, even if it can be agreed that extraterrestrial life forms are real and have visited Earth, that answer does little to clear up the mystery surrounding these beings. How do they get here in the first place?

The Problems with Space Travel

The "how" is a thorny question. In studying the universe, humanity has been able to identify certain rules that all sorts

JACQUES VALLEE

After Hynek, the most recognizable figure in the study of unidentified aerial phenomena is Jacques Vallee. Born September 24, 1939, in Pontoise, France, Vallee studied mathematics at the Sorbonne, earned a master's degree in astrophysics from the University of Lille, and a PhD in computer science in 1967 from Northwestern University in Chicago, where J. Allen Hynek was chairing the astronomy department. Today, Vallee lives in San Francisco, California, but he works around the United States on projects ranging from investment ventures for North American and European technology companies to writing award-winning science fiction and researching UFOs.

Vallee's interest in UFOs is longstanding, beginning back in France when he first observed mysterious flying phenomenon that seemed to defy human understanding of the limits of technology and the laws of physics. After he moved to America, Vallee continued to study the mysteries of space. While working for the University of Texas, he co-developed the first computerized map of Mars for NASA. Vallee later met Hynek at Northwestern, and the two worked closely together on UFO research for Project Blue Book, the name for the Air Force's project that investigated UFO reports between 1947 and 1969.

of matter follow. These are known as the **laws of physics**, and they essentially make extended space travel as we know it impossible. For example, one of these rules states that light is the fastest thing in the universe. Light is made up of photons, which are particles of matter that carry no mass, allowing them to travel at extraordinary speeds. That means that anything with mass, such as a spacecraft, must travel at a much slower rate than this. So, while it takes light, the fastest substance in the universe, radiating from Proxima Centauri (the star closest to our sun) nearly five years to reach Earth, it would take by some count seventy-six thousand years for a terrestrial vehicle to reach it. This would seem to preclude the possibility of any spacecraft from another solar system—let alone another galaxy—ever reaching Earth, right?

Well, maybe not. On the one hand, it is impossible for modern human technology, with its reliance on solid nonrenewable fuels and heavy spacecraft, to accomplish such a feat. However, our technology has been advancing at an exponential rate, increasing faster and faster as time goes on. After all, humanity put itself on the moon a little more than sixty years after developing the technology to fly. It's possible that an alien civilization on the farthest reaches of space has advanced to the point where interstellar travel is as simple

Black holes are areas of space so dense that they pull everything toward them, even light itself.

for them as it is for humans to board an overnight flight to another continent.

Masters of Time and Space

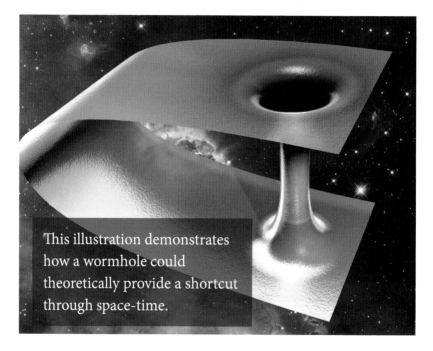

This illustration demonstrates how a wormhole could theoretically provide a shortcut through space-time.

Just as it is possible for our current understanding of technology to be limited, it is also likely that our understanding of the laws of physics is also flawed. Humanity's technological history is short; it was only relatively recently that humans proved that Earth is not flat and that it is not the center of the universe. While we might understand light to be the fastest substance in the galaxy, it is possible that we may only be working on a limited assumption about the nature of time and space. In fact, astrophysicists have already started to learn that there may be parts of the universe where those "laws" may be more like "guidelines," or may not exist at all. These areas in particular revolve around things known as black holes. Black holes are areas of space where matter is so dense and gravity is so strong that it pulls everything around it—even light—inwards. Black holes can range in size from a single atom with the mass of a mountain to so-called stellar black holes that form when a star dies and implodes. Stellar black holes have masses many times greater than our sun. Evidence suggests that our own galaxy may have a supermassive black hole at the center of it, which has over billions of years collected gases and star dust to form our galaxy.

The gravitational pull of black holes is strong enough that even light cannot escape, and it also has the effect of warping **space-time**. (Space-time is a complicated topic, but it is helpful to think of it as a fabric that can be either expanded or scrunched up, which means that distance and elapsed time can grow shorter or longer under certain circumstances.) Many scientists have argued that there is a point in a black hole called the **singularity** where matter becomes so infinitely compact that both distance and time become infinitely small. Here, "all laws of physics break down," in the words of American physicist Kip Thorne.

The singularity of a black hole may be able to support a wormhole, which is a theoretical solution to the challenges black holes pose to Albert Einstein's theory of relativity. A wormhole may act like a "shortcut" through time and space. Imagine a piece of paper with two dots on opposite ends of the same side. The two-dimensional distance between them is what separates them. Now, pick up the piece of paper and fold it so that the two points touch. The points are right on top of each other, and the shortest distance that now separates them takes place in another dimension. This is how a wormhole is imagined to function, bridging the divide between two distant expanses of space.

This theory suggests that the physics of a black hole can potentially be harnessed to allow a vehicle to travel across the expanse of space practically instantly. Granted, this is all theoretical and based on a relatively limited human understanding of the universe. However, it may help to explain why spacecraft of an extraterrestrial origin have been sighted in Earth's atmosphere for centuries, despite humanity not discovering any evidence of any sort of alien civilization in the universe. Perhaps an alien culture has been built well beyond the reach of our radios, satellites, and spacecraft, and is sophisticated enough to tap into the fundamental powers of the universe. In that case, the aliens comprising that civilization must be both old and unimaginably intelligent.

Studying Alien Abductions

Scientific investigations into cases of abductions at the hands of extraterrestrials, such as the Hill Case, remain inconclusive. For one thing, abductions are notoriously sketchy on hard evidence and complete details. Most victims of alleged abduction often only remember brief snippets of their attack, if anything at all. In many cases, the most complete accounts of abductions only come when the victim is put under hypnosis, as with Betty and Barney Hill. Those who believe that aliens are responsible for these events argue that the reason for victims' lack of memory is because they have either been traumatized by the event and their brains are therefore blocking out the complete story, or that the memories of victims have been medically altered in order to preserve the secrecy of their alien abductors. Most scientists consider these excuses to be far-fetched. For many psychologists and researchers, the reason abductees can't remember their encounters is because the encounters never happened in the first place and are instead remnants of dreams, fabrications of the imagination, or symptoms of a delusion.

THE MAN ON MARS

In July 1976, an exploration craft named *Viking 1*, observing the surface of Mars, transmitted an image that shocked the world. The orbiter seemed to have discovered a huge sculpture of a man's face, complete with eyes, nose, a mouth, and a forehead. Many alien enthusiasts argued that the striking symmetry of the features could not have formed as an accident of geology. To them, a Martian civilization must have been at work. For a brief moment, it seemed that there must be men on Mars.

The "Man on Mars"

Unfortunately for alien enthusiasts, the "Man on Mars" was confirmed to be a trick of the eye by later missions to study the surface of Mars, including the *Mars Global Surveyor* (1997–2006) and the *Mars Reconnaissance Orbiter*, which has been documenting the planet since 2006. The photos from these spacecraft were taken at a higher resolution and at different angles than the original *Viking* photo and confirm that the "face" is actually just a mountain. Its topography had been illuminated by the sun to resemble a face.

Scientists using large radio satellites such as these continue to observe the deepest parts of the universe for signs of life.

CHAPTER FIVE

Are We Alone?

I t is not outside the realm of possibility that the majority of people may be blind to a truth that is right in front of them. The world used to be flat, and people feared sailing off into uncharted waters for fear of falling off the face of the earth. People used to believe it was impossible for a heavier-than-air vehicle to fly, and later that it was impossible to travel to the moon. Today, many people assume that interstellar travel is impossible. Given all that we have been wrong about in terms of the limits of our capabilities, is it possible that this assumption will also one day, maybe soon, be proven wrong?

It is reasonable to say that our understanding of the workings of the universe is limited. We have only recently come to understand that our universe includes so much more than Earth, the sun, and other nearby planets in the solar system. We have only explored an infinitesimal corner of the universe, and much of what we think we know about galaxies, black holes, and even concepts like space and time remain highly theoretical. It is a universe of opportunity that we currently find ourselves in. No wonder many people continue to look up into the stars and ask the age-old question: Are we alone?

The Truth Is Out There

Why does the idea of extraterrestrial life continue to pop up again and again in the human imagination? Why does the possibility that life exists somewhere outside of Earth's atmosphere continue to interest and obsess people? There may be a number of answers to those questions, but it seems one reason for humanity's continued fascination with alien life centers on the fear of isolation and the need to communicate.

Gazing up at the night sky, it's obvious even with our limited understanding that the universe is a huge place, and the size of our home world is equivalent to a molecule of water in an ocean. The possibility that Earth is the only source of life in the universe can be a frightening prospect, because it might mean that the plants, animals, and people around us—and even we ourselves—are all accidental, and that everything we think we understand about those things, or about history, or about our future as a species, is all just a product of happenstance.

On the other hand, the possibility that we may not be alone carries with it hope for humanity. Hope for life. The idea that there may be another being, perhaps looking up at the stars shining down on an alien world at the same moment, wondering the same things we are, is a comfort. Maybe one day we can succeed in reaching out and making contact. Maybe we can share the best of ourselves with them and enjoy mutual benefit. And maybe when the time for life on Earth to come to a close, this civilization may carry the memory of us with them.

Today, children and adults keep searching the skies for signs of extraterrestial life.

THE WOW! SIGNAL

```
1        2          1    4
1  16    1     1
1  11    1        1       1
   1                      3
   6  2              31
1 E  4    3   12   1  21   1
  Q  1   16  1   2  1   1
  U  1    1           3  7   1
2 J  1    31  3  111    11
  5  1                 1   1
   14     1     113      2
1  3   1     1      1
1  4         1   1  1    1
   4   1  1    1  11     1
   1              1     2
1  1   1              11
   1            1
```

The year 1977 was a big one for aliens: *Star Wars* debuted in theaters, and an astronomer named Jerry Ehman working at the Ohio State University Big Ear radio telescope made an extraordinary observation. Scientists like Ehman use huge, dish-shaped radio telescopes to scan the skies for incoming radio waves. Those involved in the search for extraterrestrial life (SETI) believe that if any non-Earthling civilization were to attempt contact, they would most likely do so with radio waves, which travel at approximately the speed of light and require relatively simple technology. Practically all signals received by these telescopes have natural explanations, as a wide variety of stellar materials emit random radio signals. However, on August 15, Ehman received an unusually powerful signal, which lasted an unprecedented seventy-two seconds, coming from a grouping of stars called Chi Sagittarii. Ehman was so shocked by the signal that he wrote "*Wow!*" on the printout.

Recently, Professor Antonio Paris, who teaches astrophysics at St. Petersburg College in Florida and formerly worked for the US Department of Defense, proposed a skeptical explanation for the so-called *Wow!* signal. Paris's theory argues that the signal originated from a pair of comets that were only recently discovered and were shown to have been passing through the area Ehman was looking at the night of the signal. Both comets are surrounded by a thick cloud of hydrogen gas, which is known to emit radio waves at the exact frequency as Ehman's signal. Paris is currently looking for funding to purchase a radio telescope in order to test his hypothesis.

Despite Paris's theory, no one has yet conclusively proven what caused the *Wow!* signal, and today it remains one of the most compelling pieces of evidence for the possibility of the existence of alien life.

GLOSSARY

abduct To take someone, as by aliens, against their will.

alleged Said without proof.

close encounter An encounter with extraterrestrial life or an unidentified flying object.

conspiracy theorist A person who believes in secret plans to cover up larger events. In regards to aliens, a conspiracy theorist believes the government has attempted to conceal information about extraterrestrial life.

extraterrestrial From outside Earth's atmosphere.

galaxy A gravitational system containing billions of stars and planets along with dust and gas.

hoax An act intended to trick or dupe.

laws of physics Physical rules that apply to all matter that have been discovered by repeated experiments.

multiverse A theory of the universe that suggests our universe is actually one of many such universes neighboring one another.

pseudoscience A belief or area of study that is falsely believed to be based on science; "false science."

singularity The point in a black hole where matter becomes so infinitely compact that both distance and time become infinitely small.

skeptic A person who doubts the claims of another.

space-time The concepts of time and three-dimensional space combined into one united concept; originally proposed by Albert Einstein in his theories of relativity.

trace evidence Signs that have been discovered after an alleged event that are used to prove the event, such as fingerprints left behind at a crime scene.

UFO An acronym that stands for "unidentified flying object," which is one of a number of bodies observed in the sky that cannot be determined.

UFOlogy The study of UFOs.

FURTHER INFORMATION

Books

Hynek, J. Allen. *The UFO Experience: A Scientific Inquiry*. New York: Marlowe & Company, 1998.

Jacobsen, Annie. *Area 51: An Uncensored History of America's Top Secret Military Base*. New York: Little, Brown and Company, 2011.

Kean, Leslie. *UFOs: Generals, Pilots, and Government Officials Go on the Record*. New York: Harmony Books, 2010.

Mack, John E. *Abduction: Human Encounters with Aliens*. New York: Macmillan Publishing Company, 1994.

Websites

The History Channel: Ancient Aliens
http://www.history.com/shows/ancient-aliens
The History Channel's popular show *Ancient Aliens* explores the lore and science behind alien encounters.

The Mutual UFO Network
http://www.mufon.com
The Mutual UFO Network (MUFON) bills itself as "the world's oldest and largest UFO phenomenon investigative body."

Videos

Discovery Channel: Stephen Hawking's Into the Universe: The Wow Signal
http://www.discovery.com/tv-shows/other-shows/videos/stephen-hawkings-universe-the-wow-signal
This brief clip from *Into the Universe* with Stephen Hawking discusses the Wow! signal.

National Geographic: When Aliens Attack
http://channel.nationalgeographic.com/videos/alien-attack
This video explores the scenario of what might happen if aliens attacked Earth.

Out of the Blue: The Definitive Investigation of the UFO Phenomenon
https://www.youtube.com/watch?v=cYPCKIL7oVw
This video explores the probability that life exists on planets other than Earth and discusses cases of reported UFO sightings.

Revelation: An Exploration of the Unknown
https://www.youtube.com/watch?v=t0EYtj7FEnM&t=52s
In this video, Jack Turnbull, a lifelong believer in alien life, examines cases that seek to prove the existence of aliens in our modern world.

BIBLIOGRAPHY

"Aurora, TX Crash - 1897." MUFON.com. Accessed October 2, 2016. http://www.mufon.com/aurora-tx-crash---1897.html.

Clark, Stuart. "Alien 'Wow!' signal could be explained after almost 40 years." The Guardian.com. April 14, 2016. http://www.theguardian.com/science/across-the-universe/2016/apr/14/alien-wow-signal-could-be-explained-after-almost-40-years.

"14th April 1561: Nuremburg Celestial Phenomenon terrifies residents." April 14, 2016. http://www.historypod.net/04/14/14th-april-1561-the-nuremberg-celestial-phenomenon.

"Guide to the J. Allen Hynek (1910–1986) Papers." Northwestern University Library. Northwestern University.edu. Accessed October 2, 2016. http://findingaids.library.northwestern.edu/catalog/inu-ead-nua-archon-436.

Hynek, J. Allen. *The UFO Experience: A Scientific Inquiry.* New York: Marlowe & Company, 1998.

Jacobsen, Annie. *Area 51: An Uncensored History of America's Top Secret Military Base.* New York: Little, Brown and Company, 2011.

"How Big Is the Sun?" Berkeley.edu. Accessed October 2, 2016. http://ds9.ssl.berkeley.edu/solarweek/DISCUSSION/howbig.html.

"J. Allen Hynek's Scale of UFO Classification." The Night Sky. org. July 24, 2016. http://thenightsky.org/hynek.html.

"Jacques F. Vallee." Jacques Vallee.net. Accessed October 2, 2016. http://www.jacquesvallee.net.

"Jacques Vallee, Ph.D." UFO Researchers & People. UFO evidence.org. Accessed October 2, 2016. http://www. ufoevidence.org/researchers/detail13.htm.

Kean, Leslie. *UFOs: Generals, Pilots, and Government Officials Go on the Record.* New York: Harmony Books, 2010.

Macdonald, James. "Scientists Have an Answer to How the Egyptian Pyramids Were Built." JSTOR Daily.org. September 11, 2014. http://daily.jstor.org/scientists-have-an-answer-to-how-the-egyptian-pyramids-were-built.

Lucullus. Plutarch. Ed. Bernadotte Perrin. Tufts.edu. Accessed October 2, 2016. http://www.perseus.tufts.edu/hopper/text?doc=Plut.%20Luc.%208&lang=original.

Mack, John E. *Abduction: Human Encounters with Aliens.* New York: Macmillan Publishing Company, 1994.

Mastin, Luke. "Singularities." The Physics of the Universe.com. Accessed October 2, 2016. http://www.physicsofthe universe.com/topics_blackholes_singularities.html.

———. "Wormholes." The Physics of the Universe.com. Accessed October 2, 2016. http://www.physicsofthe universe.com/topics_blackholes.html.

Nickell, Joe. "The Story Behind the 'Alien Autopsy' Hoax." Live Science.com. May 7, 2006. http://www.livescience. com/742-story-alien-autopsy-hoax.html.

Strieber, Whitley. *Communion: A True Story*. New York: Beech Tree Books, 1987.

Thorpe, JR. "6 Famous UFO Sightings From History." Bustle. com. Accessed October 2, 2016. http://www.bustle.com/ articles/170926-6-famous-ufo-sightings-from-history.

Trussell, Robert. "The Sightings." Kansas City Theatre.com (reprinted from the *Kansas City Star*, February 17, 1985). January 13, 2012. http://kansascitytheater.wordpress.com/ tag/ufo.

Vallee, Jacques. *The Invisible College: What a Group of Scientists Has Discovered About UFO Influences on the Human Race.* New York: E. P. Dutton & Co, Inc., 1975.

Williams, Matt. "How Long Would It Take to Travel to the Nearest Star?" Universe Today.com. September 6, 2016. http://www.universetoday.com/15403/how-long-would-it-take-to-travel-to-the-nearest-star.

Wired.com Staff. "The 12 Greatest Challenges for Space Exploration." Wired.com. February 16, 2016. http://www. wired.com/2016/02/space-is-cold-vast-and-deadly-hu-mans-will-explore-it-anyway.

INDEX

Page numbers in **boldface** are illustrations. Entries in **boldface** are glossary terms.

ABOUT THE AUTHOR

Andrew Coddington has written a number of books on a wide variety of topics for Cavendish Square, including several titles in the Creatures of Fantasy series. In addition to *Aliens, UFOs, and Unexplained Encounters*, he has written *The Bermuda Triangle, Stonehenge, and Unexplained Places* and *The Hope Diamond, Cursed Objects, and Unexplained Artifacts* in the Paranormal Investigations series. He lives in Buffalo, New York, with his wife and dog.